Original title:
The Wolf's Solitude

Copyright © 2024 Swan Charm
All rights reserved.

Author: Kätriin Kaldaru
ISBN HARDBACK: 978-9908-52-554-9
ISBN PAPERBACK: 978-9908-52-555-6
ISBN EBOOK: 978-9908-52-556-3

Dreaming Amongst the Pines

In the forest where laughter rings,
Bright lights dance on the gentle springs.
With every whisper from the trees,
Joyful hearts sway in the breeze.

Candles flicker, casting warm glow,
As stars above begin to show.
Children's giggles fill the air,
In a world without a care.

A feast laid out on a blanket wide,
With sweet delights we gather side by side.
Laughter echoes, stories unfold,
In this moment, life feels bold.

As twilight paints the sky in hues,
We toast to dreams and night's good views.
With friends encircled, spirits high,
Amongst the pines, our hearts will fly.

Alone in the Embrace of the Wild

Within the forest's vibrant dance,
Colors burst, as spirits prance.
Nature sings with joyous glee,
A wild embrace, just you and me.

Sunlight filters through the trees,
Whispers ride upon the breeze.
Hearts collide with each new sound,
In this place, we're joyfully bound.

Beneath the Glistening Skies

Underneath the stars so bright,
Twinkling dreams fill up the night.
Laughter echoes, bursting free,
Unity in harmony.

Candles flicker, shadows play,
Guiding us along the way.
In this moment, spirits soar,
In our hearts, there's always more.

A Heartbeat in the Wilderness

Among the trees, the wild blooms sing,
Nature's pulse, a vibrant thing.
A whisper here, a rustle there,
In every beat, we feel the care.

Joy surrounds in every glance,
Each heartbeat joins the wild's dance.
Together lost, yet feeling found,
In wilderness, our hearts are crowned.

Beyond the Boundless Night

As shadows stretch and laughter flows,
The night unfolds, and friendship grows.
Fires crackle, stories share,
In this warmth, we cast our care.

Stars above like dreams in flight,
Guide our hopes through boundless night.
Together, we'll embrace the dark,
In unity, we kindle the spark.

Lone Howl in the Darkness

Under the moon's bright gleam,
A lone wolf finds its way,
Through shadows deep and dark,
Echoes of night softly play.

Stars twinkle high above,
A symphony of light,
Each howl a call to dance,
In the warm, festive night.

Whispering Pines

Among the towering trees,
Gentle whispers fill the air,
Leaves rustle like soft chimes,
A song of joy everywhere.

Bright lanterns sway with dreams,
Casting warmth on the ground,
Laughter blends with the breeze,
In this world, love is found.

Silent Watcher

In the glade, shadows play,
A presence, calm and pure,
Watching over celebrating hearts,
In the night, love will endure.

With each flicker of the flame,
And every joyous cheer,
The silent watcher smiles wide,
Holding memories near.

Shadows of a Forgotten Pack

Whispers of old tales linger,
In the corners of the night,
Ghosts of a time once cherished,
Dance in flickering light.

Around the fire's warm glow,
Stories rise and fall like dreams,
Amidst the shadows they roam,
In a tapestry of gleams.

Echoes in the Empty Woods

In the heart of silent trees,
Echoes of laughter blend,
A festival of spirits bright,
Where happiness has no end.

Footsteps on the forest floor,
Each one tells a tale anew,
In the empty woods, we gather,
Beneath the night's soft hue.

Where the Wild Things Roam

In fields of laughter, children play,
The sun is bright, it lights the way.
With joy they dance, and spirits soar,
In every heart, they long for more.

A gentle breeze, a playful tune,
The wild things thrive beneath the moon.
With hands held high, they jump and cheer,
Their wild adventures drawing near.

Around the fire, stories shared,
With glowing eyes, the night they dared.
In vibrant dreams, they seek to roam,
In every heart, a place called home.

Together bound, they weave their fate,
In joyous moments, love, innate.
Each wild delight, a cherished song,
In this wild land, where they belong.

An Evening's Pause in Stillness

As daylight wanes, the hues align,
A quiet peace, the stars, they shine.
In gentle whispers, night descends,
The world adorned, where magic blends.

With candles lit, the shadows dance,
Each flicker sparks a fleeting chance.
To pause and breathe, let worries cease,
In this still night, we seek our peace.

The echoes of laughter fill the air,
Moments cherished beyond compare.
With friends beside, the heart feels light,
As joy unfolds in soft twilight.

So let us pause and hold this grace,
In every smile, a warm embrace.
An evening's pause, a celebration,
Of life's pure love, our sweet creation.

Fading Footprints in the Night

Softly treads along the shore,
As waves caress and spirits soar.
With every step, a tale unfolds,
In fading tracks, the heart beholds.

The stars above, they twinkle bright,
As laughter echoes through the night.
With every glance, memories thrive,
In joyous moments, we come alive.

The gentle hum of cricket's song,
Reminds us where our hearts belong.
In fleeting dreams, we find our flight,
In fading footprints, pure delight.

Together bound by love and light,
In every pulse—our hearts unite.
With time's embrace, let sorrows cease,
In fading footprints, find our peace.

The Whispering Pines of Solitude

In quiet glades where pines stand tall,
A serenade of nature's call.
The breeze it weaves a gentle thread,
In solitude, our thoughts are fed.

With whispers soft, the shadows play,
As golden leaves drift down in sway.
Each branch a tale, each rustle sings,
In this place, the heart takes wings.

The moonlight bathes the earth in peace,
In every sigh, our worries cease.
With every breath, the spirit finds,
The solace deep within our minds.

And there beneath the starlit skies,
We learn to see with open eyes.
In whispered pines, we bid adieu,
To fleeting thoughts, embrace what's true.

The Longing of the Hidden Glen

Amidst the trees, where shadows play,
A secret whispers, beckons to stay.
Colors dance in sunlight's glow,
A place of magic, only we know.

Laughter echoes, hearts entwined,
In the glen, joy is defined.
Breezes carry sweet perfume,
The world outside fades like a plume.

Moonlight drapes a silver thread,
While dreams awaken in our head.
Together here, we lose all care,
In sacred moments, rich and rare.

So let us wander, hand in hand,
In the hidden glen, a timeless land.
Where every leaf a story spun,
And festal hearts beat as one.

Silence Treads Softly on Old Trails

Gentle echoes of days gone by,
Soft whispers of the wind draw nigh.
The sun spills gold on ancient stones,
While nature's choir hums in tones.

Crisp leaves crunch beneath our feet,
With every step, our hearts repeat.
Joy lies in the simple sound,
Of silence treading on hallowed ground.

Dreams awaken in twilight's glow,
As stars emerge in evening's show.
Together we weave tales of glee,
While the old trails cradle you and me.

In the hush of night, friends gather near,
A festivity sparked by cheer.
With laughter echoing through the pines,
In these still moments, our joy aligns.

An Ethereal Lament

In twilight's grasp, the shadows sigh,
Whispers of heartbeats, dreams nearby.
Misty veils where laughter flares,
An ethereal lament fills the airs.

Stars wink playfully, secrets shared,
While moonlight spills, our souls bared.
In the stillness, a haunting tune,
Festive echoes beneath the moon.

Reviving memories, tender and sweet,
In the soft glow, we feel complete.
With every note, our spirits rise,
In harmony, under starlit skies.

So let the night wrap us tight,
With joyous tears, we embrace the light.
While the ethereal echoes and bend,
We come together, hearts to mend.

The Path Untrodden and Wild

Upon the brink of the wild unknown,
A path awaits, where seeds are sown.
With every step, anticipation grows,
A festivity pure, as wonder flows.

Sun-kissed petals, butterflies soar,
Nature's canvas forevermore.
Together we wander, hand in hand,
On the untrodden path, we make our stand.

Chasing whispers of the wandering breeze,
In the wild, our spirits ease.
While laughter dances in the air,
The joy of existence is ours to share.

So here we dance, beneath the trees,
With hearts uplifted, always at ease.
As the sun sets, golden and bright,
We celebrate love, in pure delight.

Solace in the Howling Wind

Beneath the stars, we gather near,
With laughter bright, we shun all fear.
The wind it howls, a joyful sound,
In this embrace, our hearts are found.

Colors dance in lantern light,
As we share stories of the night.
The music plays, and spirits soar,
Each note a whisper, forevermore.

With every cheer and gleeful song,
Together here, where we belong.
In festive joy, we raise a toast,
To friendships true, we love the most.

So let the winds blow wild and free,
For in their song, we find our glee.
In this sweet moment, time stands still,
As laughter echoes, hearts to fill.

Eyes of the Solitary Night

Beneath the watchful moon's soft gaze,
The night unfolds in secret ways.
With shadows long and whispers low,
A magic stirs, and feelings grow.

In solitude, the stars we find,
Each twinkle speaks to heart and mind.
A hint of joy in the still air,
A festive spirit lingers there.

We dance among the midnight blooms,
As fragrant dreams dispel our glooms.
The world outside fades far away,
In this embrace, we wish to stay.

So let the night be ours to keep,
With gentle laughter in our sleep.
For in this quiet, we ignite
The wonders born of solitude's light.

Wistful Gaze Under the Silver Moon

Underneath the silver glow,
A wistful gaze, our hearts in tow.
The night wraps round like velvet cloth,
With hopes and dreams, we dare to quoth.

Festive lights in laughter's throng,
A melody that feels so strong.
With every glance, a story told,
In this sweet light, we find our gold.

The moonbeams dance on faces bright,
As we celebrate this wondrous night.
With fleeting time, we slow our pace,
In joy, we find our rightful place.

So let us cherish seconds near,
With every smile, let's conquer fear.
In ambiance of love and cheer,
We weave our memories, crystal clear.

Between Ridges and Echoing Calls

Amidst the ridges, voices blend,
In echoing calls, our hearts extend.
With laughter bright and spirits bold,
We gather here, in joy untold.

The festive air is rich with cheer,
As friends unite, we draw them near.
With tales of old and futures bright,
Together we ignite the night.

Beneath the moon's soft, watchful eyes,
We let our worries drift and rise.
In every leap and joyful sound,
A deeper bond in love is found.

So here between the hills we stand,
With open hearts, and outstretched hand.
Echoes of laughter fill the sky,
In this celebration, we will fly.

Streams of Distant Echoes

The laughter bubbles in the air,
Bright colors swirl without a care.
Candles flicker, whispers blend,
Hope and joy, a joyful trend.

Echoes of music fill the street,
Families gather, share the heat.
Togetherness rings in each heart,
In this moment, we won't part.

Fireworks painting the night sky,
Lighting dreams as they soar high.
Together we dance, we sing loud,
In the magic, we are proud.

With smiles shining in the light,
We embrace the warm delight.
These streams of laughter ever flow,
Underneath the evening glow.

To Be at One with the Shadows

Whispers of joy in dim-lit halls,
Dancing softly as twilight calls.
Candles flicker in warm embrace,
Embracing shadows, a sacred space.

The air is filled with sweet perfume,
As laughter mingles with the gloom.
In the corners, secrets sigh,
To be at one, just you and I.

The moonlight casts its gentle rays,
Guiding us through shadowed ways.
We twirl 'neath stars, our spirits free,
Lost in moments, just you and me.

With every laugh, a bond we weave,
In this night, we'll never grieve.
To revel in the dark's embrace,
Together we'll find our hidden grace.

A Dance of Solitary Flames

In the quiet of night, flames arise,
Each flicker tells its own surprise.
Alone yet bright, they dance and sway,
Igniting dreams in a unique way.

Circles swirl and shadows beckon,
Through the dark, we find connection.
A rhythm pulsing, wild and free,
Each ember whispers, 'Come dance with me.'

Twinkling lights in a sea of night,
Casting warmth with their soft light.
Each solitary flame a voice,
In their glow, our hearts rejoice.

So come, take part in this timeless game,
Together we spark, never the same.
In the dance of flames, we find our place,
Each flickering soul, a warm embrace.

Underneath a Blanket of Stars

Underneath a blanket, stars so bright,
We gather close in the warm twilight.
Laughter mingles with the gentle breeze,
As fireflies twinkle among the trees.

Whispers of dreams are softly said,
With every heartache, we're better led.
The night holds promise, wild and rare,
In this moment, we lose all care.

Songs rise up to the moonlit dome,
In this garden, we find our home.
Each sparkling light, a tale to share,
Connected by love, drifting in air.

As constellations weave their dance,
Together we lose ourselves in chance.
Underneath a sky, vast and deep,
We cherish this night; our hearts will keep.

Silent Vigil Beneath the Stars

Under the glow of evening lights,
Laughter dances through the night.
Colors swirl, joy takes flight,
Beneath the stars, all feels right.

Fires crackle, warmth embraces,
Smiles bloom on familiar faces.
Songs of joy echo through the air,
Togetherness, a treasured affair.

The moon, a lantern, guiding all,
In this moment, we stand tall.
Hearts united, spirits soar,
In this vigil, we want more.

As the world fades into dreams,
Festive hearts burst at the seams.
With every cheer and every song,
In this night, we all belong.

Sorrow of the Howling Night

Beneath the moon, shadows creep,
Whispers echo, secrets deep.
The howl of winds sings a tune,
Sadness dances with the moon.

Lost in thoughts of what has been,
A heart heavy, a silent sin.
Yet in the darkness, a spark ignites,
Hope twinkles in the sorrowed nights.

Ghostly figures move with grace,
Remnants of a forgotten space.
Still, amidst the chilling fright,
Resilience blooms in the night.

For even in the darkest hour,
Life knows how to find its power.
A bittersweet, festive cheer,
This howling night can still endear.

Wanderer's Lament on Frosted Ground

Through frosted fields, a wanderer treads,
Whispers of stories beneath the threads.
Each step a memory, soft and light,
Wrapped in the blanket of chilly night.

Stars twinkle like diamonds in the sky,
Every glimmer a heartfelt sigh.
The chill brings a festive air,
Even loneliness finds warmth somewhere.

Echoes of laughter from distant halls,
Invite the wanderer as night falls.
A fleeting joy, though bittersweet,
In this journey, the heart finds beat.

Yet as frost carpets the ground,
A melody of hope is found.
In the silence, joy's refrain,
A festive spirit in the pain.

Hidden in the Thicket of Night

In the thicket, shadows play,
Dreams linger as night hues sway.
Festive whispers rustle the leaves,
Nature's song among the eves.

Stars peek through branches with grace,
Illuminating this secret space.
A gathering of hearts, unseen,
Where joy and magic weave a scene.

The rustling leaves a joyful cue,
Beneath the sky, a different view.
In the night, our spirits dance,
Every moment, a touched chance.

Hidden laughter fills the air,
In this thicket, we lay bare.
With every beat, our souls take flight,
Together, basking in the night.

Solitary Steps on Crimson Leaves

Crimson leaves dance on the breeze,
Autumn whispers through the trees.
A lone step echoes, soft and sweet,
In this moment, life feels complete.

Golden sunlight paints the ground,
In every corner, joy is found.
Laughter floats on the amber air,
Celebration, everywhere!

Beneath the branches, shadows play,
As nature hums a festive sway.
Each crunch of leaves beneath my feet,
A symphony, oh so elite.

With every stride, the heart expands,
Connected here, no need for plans.
In solitude, but not alone,
In every leaf, love's spirit shone.

A Distant Cry for Connection

A distant cry upon the wind,
Echoing where the night begins.
Stars above twinkle with delight,
Inviting all to share the night.

A flicker of hope lights the sky,
Whispers of joy that soar and fly.
Every heartbeat seeks a friend,
In unity, our dreams ascend.

From shadows deep, a laughter breaks,
In every smile, a memory wakes.
Bound by the threads of shared laughter,
We dance to the song of ever after.

So raise a glass to joys untold,
To stories shared, to hearts of gold.
In this festivity, we find,
That love connects all humankind.

The Silent Path of Shadows

On the path where shadows play,
Underneath the moon's soft ray.
Whispers linger, gentle and light,
With every step, the world feels right.

Starlit skies above us gleam,
Filling the night with vibrant dreams.
A secret dance begins to unfold,
In the shadows, our tales are told.

Sounds of laughter fill the air,
A melody, beyond compare.
In the silence, joy is found,
As hearts unite, no bounds around.

So tread lightly on this ground,
In the echo of joy's profound.
Together, we weave our fates,
In this silent world that celebrates.

Tales of the Wanderer's Heart

A wanderer's heart beats free and bold,
Seeking stories yet untold.
With every journey taken wide,
A festival of joy inside.

Mountains high and valleys deep,
In every corner, memories keep.
Through bustling streets and quiet lanes,
The spirit of life forever reigns.

With friends beside and laughter loud,
In every moment, we feel proud.
Together weaving tales of old,
In celebration, hearts unfold.

So lift your voice, let it resound,
In the tales where love is found.
For every step upon this earth,
Is a testament of our worth.

Memory Like an Unfolding Map

Colors dance like whispers bright,
In every fold, a day ignites.
Joyful laughter fills the air,
As moments fade without a care.

Maps of yesteryears are drawn,
With paths where dreams are gently born.
Each line connects a cherished face,
Along this route, we find our place.

Wondrous stories gleam and sway,
With every bend, they find their way.
Echoes of the past resound,
In the joy where love is found.

The festive spirit finds its spark,
In memories that light the dark.
With friends beside in radiant glee,
A map unfolds—our hearts fly free.

Lost among the Echoes of Time

In the forest, whispers swell,
Secrets hidden, tales to tell.
Echoes dance in vibrant hues,
Beneath the canopy of blues.

Each footstep finds a rhythm sweet,
As moments gather, hearts repeat.
Lost among the rustling leaves,
A fest of joy that never grieves.

Time meanders, lets us roam,
In every shadow, we feel at home.
Songs of laughter ride the breeze,
And memories float among the trees.

With every heartbeat, joy unfolds,
In radiant shades, our story molds.
The echoing past, a festive chime,
We find ourselves, lost in time.

The Solitude of Wind-Swept Hills

On hills where whispers greet the sky,
The wind tells tales that never die.
Each gust brings life, a jubilant cheer,
In solitude, we feel them near.

With meadows bright and skies so wide,
The festive spirit, our hearts abide.
Dancing shadows play on grass,
As fleeting moments come to pass.

The solitude wraps us in grace,
With every breath, we find our place.
Hills adorned in nature's light,
A symphony of day and night.

Celebrate the gentle sway,
Of wind and laughter on display.
In every breath, the joy instills,
A festive warmth on wind-swept hills.

A Heart Adrift in Wilderness

In the wild, where colors blend,
A heart adrift begins to mend.
Nature's chorus sings so sweet,
With each new path, our souls compete.

Through fields alive in sunlit cheer,
We find our way, our dreams are clear.
A mosaic of moments unfolds,
In wilderness, sweet stories told.

With gentle streams and skies so bright,
The festive glow ignites the night.
Each rustling leaf, a dance divine,
In perfect harmony, we intertwine.

Wander free where spirits soar,
In wilderness, we crave for more.
A heart once lost finds love and fire,
In festive joy, we lift higher.

A Canvas of Dusk and Dreams

As twilight paints the evening sky,
Colors blend and softly sigh.
Laughter dances in the air,
Whispers of joy, everywhere.

With lanterns glowing, hearts ignite,
Embracing warmth, the stars are bright.
Every face, a story told,
In this moment, memories unfold.

The music swells, the spirits rise,
Underneath the tapestry of skies.
We gather close, with hands entwined,
In this canvas, love defined.

So let the laughter never cease,
In these moments, find your peace.
The dusk holds dreams, both vast and grand,
A joyful heart, take a stand.

The Call Before the Dawn

In the hush of night's embrace,
Echoes of hope begin to trace.
Stars like lanterns flicker bright,
Guiding dreams into the light.

Voices whisper through the mist,
Melodies of joy persist.
Each heartbeat sings a brand new song,
A symphony where we belong.

The world awaits with bated breath,
To greet the dawn, to dance with zest.
Shadows fade as colors bloom,
In the morning, life resumes.

So take a moment, breathe it in,
Feel the magic, let it spin.
For every ending we have known,
Is but the seed from which we've grown.

Reflections of a Wandering Spirit

As rivers flow, our stories blend,
Through valleys deep, we wander, friends.
Every path, a tale to share,
In the whispers of the air.

Mountains high and oceans wide,
In nature's arms, we take a ride.
Each horizon holds a dream,
A tapestry, a vibrant theme.

We dance beneath the twilight glow,
Embracing freedom as we go.
With every step, our spirits soar,
In the voyage, we find more.

So raise a glass to journeys passed,
To moments cherished, too quick to last.
With open hearts, we'll roam and sing,
Celebrating what each day will bring.

The Solitary Brush of Nature

With gentle strokes, the forest breathes,
Upon its canvas, life weaves.
Colors flourish, bold and bright,
In nature's arms, pure delight.

Whispers of the wind entwine,
Each leaf a story, simply divine.
The sun peeks through the leafy lace,
A radiant smile on nature's face.

Brooks babble tales of yesteryear,
Echoes of laughter draw us near.
In solitude, we find our song,
In the heart of nature, we belong.

So pause awhile in nature's grace,
Let your spirit find its place.
A solitary brush, serene and clear,
Paints our joys, captures cheer.

Spirits of the Midnight Trail

Beneath the stars where shadows play,
The spirits dance in bright array,
With laughter ringing through the night,
They guide our souls to pure delight.

A fire crackles, warmth surrounds,
With every cheer, a joy abounds,
Their whispers fold us in a dream,
As moonbeams cast a silver gleam.

The midnight trail, a path so bright,
Leads us to a joyful height,
In every heart, the revels soar,
For festive spirits we adore.

So raise a glass to friends so dear,
In merriment, we banish fear,
Together here, our hearts entwine,
In midnight's glow, we'll always shine.

Lonesome Song Among the Pines

A lonesome song among the pines,
Where echoes of the past entwines,
The melody of winds will sway,
As memories dance and drift away.

Beneath their boughs, a tale unfolds,
Of whispered secrets, brave and bold,
Each note that rises in the breeze,
Brings forth a warmth that longs to please.

The forest hums a joyous tune,
As lanterns light beneath the moon,
In every shadow, laughter swells,
The heart, it knows where solace dwells.

So gather 'round, let spirits flow,
With every strum, the feelings grow,
We sing together, bond we find,
In lonesome songs, we are combined.

An Evening's Remorse

An evening's glow, a bittersweet,
Where memories of love repeat,
The stars above like candles gleam,
As wistful hearts begin to dream.

For moments lost in time's embrace,
We cherish every sweet-filled space,
Yet shadows linger, soft regret,
In festive lights, our hearts forget.

A gentle sigh escapes the lips,
As laughter dances, joy eclipsed,
But in our eyes, a spark ignites,
A hope renewed in fading nights.

So let us toast to fleeting time,
In every beat, a tender rhyme,
For even in the darkest days,
The festive spirit finds its ways.

Driftwood Dreams in Creeping Fog

In creeping fog, the driftwood lies,
With stories whispered, soft goodbyes,
A festive cheer in silence hides,
As nature's wonders gently bide.

The ocean's breeze brings life anew,
In swirling mist, the dreams break through,
Like flickering flames that warm the night,
Each moment captured, pure delight.

Among the sands, we build and play,
Their laughter echoes, come what may,
With each wave crashing, joy will swell,
In driftwood dreams, all's well that dwells.

So raise your voice to skies above,
In festival of life and love,
For in the fog, our spirits soar,
Embracing dreams forevermore.

The Call of the Wandering Night

Beneath the stars, we sway and sing,
The moon invites, its silver ring.
Laughter echoes through the trees,
As night embraces, hearts at ease.

Whispers float on breezy sails,
The sound of joy in festive trails.
With every step, our spirits soar,
We dance beneath the night's grand door.

Flickering lights like fireflies dance,
In this moment, we take a chance.
Together under skies so bright,
We heed the call of wandering night.

So raise your glass, let voices blend,
As friendships bloom that never end.
A celebration, wild and free,
In this enchanted jubilee.

Solitude's Song in the Twilight

As twilight paints the world in gold,
A melody of dreams unfolds.
With echoes soft that call my name,
Solitude wraps me, gently tame.

The candles flicker, shadows play,
In this hour, magic finds its way.
Each note a whisper, sweet and clear,
A song of solace, drawing near.

With every chord, the heart takes flight,
In solitude's embrace tonight.
The world outside may drift away,
In twilight's arms, we choose to stay.

Together here, though miles apart,
Each strum unites the wandering heart.
As stars awaken, dreams ignite,
We find our peace in twilight's light.

The Scent of Distant Memories

In the air, a fragrance sweet,
Tales of old and moments fleet.
A hint of laughter, days gone by,
The scent of love, it makes me sigh.

With every breath, the past returns,
A whisper of the heart that yearns.
The cinnamon and pine aligned,
Bring forth the memories entwined.

In joyful times, we shared our dreams,
With every sunset, life redeems.
The warmth of hearth, the friends we find,
In fleeting scents, our souls rewind.

So let us cherish all we've known,
In every fragrance, we have grown.
With gratitude, we reminisce,
In distant memories, we find bliss.

A Journey Beyond the Howling Winds

Through howling winds, we make our way,
With hearts on fire, come what may.
Adventure calls, we heed its cry,
With spirits high, we touch the sky.

The world unfolds, a vibrant hue,
In every corner, something new.
Together we will pave the road,
Each step a tale, a life bestowed.

The mountains rise, the rivers flow,
In nature's arms, our dreams we sow.
With laughter loud and voices bright,
We'll find our path in the moonlight.

Through storm and calm, our journey's sweet,
In every moment, life's a treat.
No howling winds can dim our flame,
For joy is ours, forever the same.

The Lament of the Lone Traveler

In the midst of laughter and song,
A solitary figure walks on,
Wishing for joy to fill the air,
Yet finding solace in silence there.

Bright lanterns glow in the night's embrace,
While others sway in a merry chase,
The stars above twinkle like cheer,
But the traveler holds a fading tear.

Voices blend in a rhythmic cheer,
Each note shimmering, so sincere,
With every step, the heart does ache,
Longing for bonds, fragile and fake.

Yet amidst the warmth of festive glee,
A whisper calls from within the sea,
The lone traveler paints dreams anew,
In the fading hues, hope shines through.

In Search of Echoes Long Abandoned

Through bustling streets where laughter flows,
A seeker wanders, where no one knows,
Chasing shadows of voices past,
In corners where memories are cast.

Bright markets hum with life so sweet,
Yet the heart craves the absent beat,
Gone are the echoes of days gone by,
Replaced by the drone of a summer sigh.

Festive colors paint every stall,
But the chronicler hears a distant call,
Of whispered dreams and fleeting time,
Beneath the surface, a haunting rhyme.

As lanterns twinkle in the night sky,
The seeker breathes a wistful sigh,
For echoes linger in hidden halls,
Remnants of laughter adorned with thralls.

The Solace of Silent Woods

In the heart of the woods, where secrets thrive,
Festivities fade, and spirits arrive,
Beneath the boughs, a gentle grace,
Laughter dances in this sacred space.

The rustle of leaves hums a sweet tune,
While shadows shift beneath the moon,
With every breeze, the whispers play,
A harmony softens the edge of day.

Among the trees, the world feels bright,
In this festive calm, all hearts unite,
Nature's embrace, a joyful retreat,
Where silence echoes, and souls can meet.

With candlelight flickering, spirits soar,
The woods hold tales from days of yore,
In the solace found, we all can share,
A festive peace woven with care.

Where Shadows Dance with the Dusk

As twilight falls, the colors burst,
In shadows deep, where dreams can thrust,
Beneath the sigh of the evening glow,
Festive spirits begin to flow.

Whirls of laughter spin in the breeze,
While fireflies flitter among the trees,
Each flicker a sign of light's embrace,
In every shadow, a familiar face.

Drums begin to echo through the night,
Celebrations rise, a wondrous sight,
With every heartbeat, the dance ignites,
Merging joy and magic in festive flights.

Where dusk meets dawn in colors bold,
Tales of old and new unfold,
As shadows swirl in a midnight trance,
We find our rhythm in the dance.

A Yearning Heart's Soliloquy

In the glow of twilight's grace,
A heart beats quick, a joyful pace.
Songs of laughter fill the air,
With every cheer, we shed our care.

Candles flicker, shadows dance,
Lost in the magic, we take a chance.
Voices rise like stars above,
A symphony of warmth and love.

Glimmers of hope in every gaze,
Together we bask in festive rays.
Whispers of dreams beneath the night,
We celebrate this pure delight.

As we gather, spirits high,
Underneath the cosmic sky.
A yearning heart, forever free,
In this moment, endlessly.

Remnants of a Brotherhood Past.

Through the years, we've shared our tales,
In laughter loud and gusty gales.
Echoes of joy, a brotherhood's might,
Together we shine, like stars at night.

Old photographs, a treasure trove,
Memories cherished, forever wove.
Raise a glass to the bonds we've made,
In the warmth of night, our fears allayed.

Voices blend like a lively tune,
Beneath the watchful, humming moon.
Each story a thread in fellowship spun,
Remnants of nights filled with fun.

As the flames crackle, shadows play,
We find our hearts, come what may.
Together we stand, strong and free,
In the tapestry of camaraderie.

Moonlit Echoes of a Feral Heart

Underneath the glimmering sky,
Wild hearts dance, let spirits fly.
Beneath the moon's enchanting glow,
Feral whispers begin to flow.

Trees sway gently, secrets shared,
Every pulse of nature bared.
With laughter bright, we twirl and spin,
The night calls out, let the revelry begin.

Fires crackle, stories ignite,
In the shadows, we embrace the night.
In this moment, wild and true,
Moonlit echoes pull me to you.

As the stars join in our spree,
We are forever, wild and free.
Feral hearts, each beat our own,
In this joyous realm, we have grown.

Shadows Whisper Through the Pines

Through the woods, the shadows creep,
In festive nights, secrets they keep.
A chorus of rustles, soft and light,
Whispers of joy steadily ignite.

Lanterns gleam like fireflies,
Painting the night with glowing ties.
Beneath the pines, a gathering throng,
In the heartbeat of night, we belong.

Laughter breaks, a soothing balm,
In the cool hush, we find our calm.
Shadows dance with flickering glee,
In the embrace of mystery.

As we share dreams 'neath silver leaves,
The spirit of festivity weaves.
Together we rise, hearts entwined,
In the shadows, our dreams aligned.

The Silent Guardian of the Night

Stars twinkle gently, lights of cheer,
Whispers of joy drift close and near.
The moon glows softly, a watchful eye,
Guiding our dreams as the hours fly.

Laughter dances on the crisp night air,
Fires crackle with warmth, hearts laid bare.
Friends gather round, sharing tales unsaid,
Wrapped in the magic, we laugh and tread.

Banners of light wave through the trees,
Nature's orchestra hums with a breeze.
Every shadow holds a secret light,
In this embrace of the silent night.

So raise a glass to the stars above,
In the night's arms, we find our love.
Together we shine, a luminous sight,
As we dance with joy in the guardian's light.

Twilight's Embrace of the Untamed

In the twilight hour, the wildflowers bloom,
Nature's playground dispels all gloom.
Colors collide in a vibrant display,
Inviting all creatures to join the fray.

Laughter echoes amidst the tall trees,
As fireflies gather, flashing with ease.
The night beckons with its mystical call,
A celebration waits, come one, come all.

With every heartbeat, the rhythm grows strong,
In the heart of the wild, we all belong.
The untamed spirit dances and sways,
In twilight's embrace, we lose count of days.

Beneath the sky as the stars ignite,
Together we bask in the sheer delight.
With every whisper, a promise we make,
To cherish this moment, for memory's sake.

Through the Thicket of Isolation

Through dense thickets, we wander free,
Casting aside all our worry and plea.
Each rustle and sigh gives way to a song,
Uniting our spirits, growing strong.

The festive air swells with joyous delight,
Bringing together hearts within sight.
In the isolation, community gleams,
As laughter and cheer weave through our dreams.

Lanterns glow softly, lighting the way,
Guiding our hearts through the drift of the day.
The thicket, a shelter, where friendships ignite,
Blossoming colors in soft, gentle light.

So let us embrace all that life has to give,
In moments of revelry, together we live.
Through thickets of challenges, we rise and we sing,
In this festive spirit, we find our own wing.

Beneath the Gaze of an Old Moon

Beneath the old moon, stories untold,
Sparkle like diamonds, glimmering bold.
In its silver gaze, we gather our dreams,
Together we weave joyful light streams.

The night wraps around, a comforting cloak,
Laughter and warmth in each word that we spoke.
The echoes of friendships, like stars, align,
Illuminating paths that forever entwine.

As shadows retreat, and the night claims its throne,
We dance in the magic, never alone.
Each heartbeat a rhythm, the world spins in tune,
Under the watchful, wise gaze of the moon.

So let us celebrate, beneath its embrace,
In unity's comfort, we each find our place.
With spirits uplifted, we revel with cheer,
In the glow of the moon, our hearts feel no fear.

Moonlit Descent into Stillness

Under the glow of a silver moon,
Whispers of night hum a soft tune.
Laughter and joy dance in the air,
As dreams take flight from the depths of care.

Crisp air sparkles with magic bright,
Embracing the warmth of festive light.
In shadows, the stories come alive,
As hearts rejoice and spirits thrive.

With each twinkling star, hopes ignite,
In this serene, enchanting night.
Together we savor the moments near,
As the embrace of stillness draws us here.

Moonlit descents bring peace anew,
In this wonderland, we're me and you.
A tapestry woven with laughter and cheer,
In the stillness of night, all is clear.

Tracks in the Fresh Snow

Footprints shimmer on the soft white sheet,
Each step a memory, a joy bittersweet.
Children's laughter weaves through the trees,
As winter's chill wraps around with ease.

Hot cocoa warms our chilly hands,
While snowflakes swirl in enchanted bands.
The world transformed under a bright sun,
In this festive dance, we all are one.

Glistening paths beckon us to explore,
The beauty of winter, a grand folklore.
With every heartbeat, we sing and play,
Creating moments that forever stay.

With each passing hour, the joy does grow,
In this season of love, let the laughter flow.
Fresh snow before us, a canvas so wide,
In tracks we leave, our spirits abide.

A Heartbeat Beneath the Stars

Beneath the vast, twinkling dome above,
Fires flicker with warmth and love.
Stories shared under the night's embrace,
As we find harmony in this sacred space.

Each heartbeat echoes through the night,
Drawing us closer, igniting delight.
Laughter sparkles as bright as the sky,
In the vast expanse, our spirits fly.

With every wish cast upon the breeze,
Hope intertwines with the rustling trees.
In the cool night air, magic does bloom,
As stars wink down, dispelling the gloom.

Together we stand, hearts open wide,
In this festive moment, joy is our guide.
A heartbeat beneath, so alive and so free,
In the melody of friendship, just you and me.

Ghost of the Untamed Forest

In the heart of woods where shadows play,
Ghostly whispers roam and sway.
Festive echoes rustle through the pines,
As nature's beauty in mystery shines.

With lanterns glowing like fireflies,
We weave through places where enchantment lies.
The spirit of joy dances with the breeze,
Among whispering leaves, we find our ease.

Ancient trees hold stories untold,
Crafting a narrative both deep and bold.
As laughter rings out in the moonlit air,
The ghostly realm of the forest is fair.

In the untamed wild, our hearts take flight,
Finding solace in the calm of the night.
With whispers of joy, we dwell and smile,
In the ghost of the forest, we linger awhile.

An Ode to the Untamed Soul

In fields of wildflowers, we dance,
With laughter that echoes, a vibrant chance.
The sun paints our faces, oh, what a show,
Embracing the freedom that comes with the flow.

With every sweet whisper, our spirits take flight,
Chasing the moments that shimmer with light.
The world is a canvas, our hearts are the brush,
In the heartbeat of joy, there's never a rush.

Together we gather, a luminous stream,
In the warmth of connection, we weave a dream.
The music, it swells, as night starts to fall,
Untamed and unwritten, we answer the call.

So raise up your voices, in harmony bright,
For the untamed soul, let us celebrate night.
With colors of wonder and laughter so bold,
An ode to the spirit, forever untold.

Fables of the Nightwalker

In the hush of the twilight, tales come alive,
Of nightwalkers wandering, where shadows thrive.
With stars as their lanterns, they dance through the dark,
Whispering secrets, igniting a spark.

Around the old bonfire, stories unfold,
Of journeys through realms that shimmer like gold.
Their laughter spills freely, like wine in a glass,
Echoing softly as moments all pass.

With shadows as partners, and dreams in their grasp,
The night is a fable, in its tender clasp.
They twirl through the air, like leaves in the breeze,
Sharing their wonders with infinite ease.

So gather together, under moon's gentle gaze,
For fables of nightwalkers, in this joyous haze.
Their stories will linger, like stars in the sky,
In the dance of the night, our spirits can fly.

The Wanderer's Heartbeat

To wander is to live, free as the breeze,
With every new pathway, the heart finds its ease.
Each footstep a promise, each glance a new start,
In dance with the world, the wanderer's heart.

With laughter as compass, and joy as the map,
We chase after sunsets, in the glow of the gap.
With friends on the journey, each moment's a song,
In the rhythm of life, we can never go wrong.

Through mountains and valleys, our spirits will soar,
In the tapestry woven, we're never ignored.
The music of nature, it calls from afar,
The wanderer's heartbeat, a bright shining star.

So gather your dreams, let the adventure unfold,
With the wanderer's spirit, be brave and be bold.
For life is a journey, a festival bright,
In the dance of existence, we revel in light.

Solitude Beneath Starlit Canopies

In the hush of the forest, beneath the tall trees,
Solitude whispers, carried by the breeze.
With starlight to guide us, we find our own way,
In the dance of the night, let our spirits play.

The moon paints a canvas of silvery dreams,
In stillness, we gather, as quiet light gleams.
With shadows as friends, and the night as our cloak,
We breathe in the magic, in silence we soak.

Through the heart of the cosmos, our thoughts intertwine,

With whispers of wonders, our souls brightly shine.
In solitude wrapped, there's a festival glow,
As the universe sings of the love it can show.

So linger a while in this delicate peace,
Beneath starlit canopies, let worries cease.
For in the embrace of the night, we are whole,
Solitude dances, igniting the soul.

The Forgotten Trails of Memory

Laughter echoes where we used to roam,
Bright colors dance in twilight's soft glow.
Memories flash like fireflies at night,
Every moment cherished, a radiant show.

The trails once traveled, now overgrown,
Yet whispers of joy linger in the breeze.
We gather together, hearts like the sun,
In festive spirit, our minds find ease.

Each song we share brings the past to life,
In stories told, and dreams we ignite.
Under twinkling stars, our spirits rise,
The forgotten trails shine, gleaming so bright.

So let us dance on this hallowed ground,
Revel in moments that time cannot steal.
With open hearts, let our laughter ring,
In the joyful warmth, we all truly feel.

In the Shadow of Ancient Trees

Beneath the boughs that touch the sky,
Our voices blend with the rustling leaves.
In laughter and cheer, the echoes fly,
As twilight weaves tales that nature weaves.

The ancient trees cradle our joyous hearts,
In their shade, we find solace and cheer.
With every festival, each friend imparts,
A bond of connection that we hold dear.

We celebrate life with each sparkling toast,
Underneath the veils of the silken green.
In this sacred grove, we cherish the most,
The spirit of friendship, forever unseen.

As shadows grow long, the night starts to play,
The stars come alive, a breathtaking sight.
In the shadow of trees, we sing and we sway,
Together forever, in pure delight.

Echoing Footsteps on Lost Paths

Step by step, we wander free,
On paths that twist through memories old.
Each echoing footstep, a melody,
In the vibrant tales of those we hold.

With lanterns lit and smiles aglow,
We chase the night with laughter and song.
Through whispers of shadows, we gently flow,
Connecting our hearts where we all belong.

Each turn, a surprise, new wonders unfold,
The night is alive, with magic so real.
With stories shared, our spirits are bold,
In this festive realm, we dance and we feel.

So let the stars guide our weary feet,
On lost paths we tread, with joy intertwined.
In every heartbeat, a rhythm so sweet,
Together forever, eternally signed.

An Oracle of the Silver Moon

Under a sky of shimmering dreams,
The silver moon casts a luminous glow.
With whispers of magic in the moonbeams,
An oracle calls us to dance and to flow.

In circles we gather, our hearts in a flame,
The laughter that twinkles like stars in the dark.
Embracing the night, we celebrate name,
In tales of old, we ignite the spark.

The moonlight unveils our hopes and our fears,
As we spin in delight, let the rhythm take hold.
With every pulse, we cast off our tears,
In the warmth of the circle, our spirits unfold.

As the night deepens, let melodies soar,
An oracle speaks in the whispers of light.
With joy in our hearts, we always want more,
Under the silver moon, everything feels right.

Musings of an Isolated Heart

In twilight's glow, whispers soar,
Beneath the stars, spirits roar.
Laughter echoes through the trees,
Joyful hearts dance in the breeze.

With radiant smiles, we unite,
Under the moon's soft, gentle light.
Celebration fills the night air,
In each moment, love we share.

Drums beat wild, and voices sing,
Life's a tapestry, joy we bring.
Emotions soar, pure and bright,
Together we paint the night.

So raise a glass, let worries cease,
In this revelry, find sweet peace.
An isolated heart now knows,
In festivity, true love grows.

The Veil of Night's Solitude

Beneath the stars, shadows play,
Soft whispers tell of night's ballet.
Silken dreams in a gentle trance,
The moonlight beckons, come and dance.

Crickets sing their lullabies,
While fireflies flash like tiny sighs.
In this stillness, hope takes flight,
A canvas bright with pure delight.

Each heartbeat sways with nature's tune,
Embracing life beneath the moon.
A festive air in solitude,
Connecting hearts with gratitude.

So let the night weave its spell,
In quiet revelry, we dwell.
Together under the starry dome,
In night's embrace, we find our home.

Reflections in a Still Creek

Mirrored waters glisten bright,
Ripples dance in pure delight.
Nature's canvas, colors blend,
In every glance, a life to mend.

Children's laughter fills the air,
Sunshine warmth, beyond compare.
With every step, the journey flows,
In every heart, a story grows.

Beneath the boughs, picnics spread,
Whispers of joy and love are fed.
Together we savor every bite,
In this moment, all feels right.

A tapestry woven of dreams,
As friendship flows like silver streams.
In reflections bright and clear,
Festivities thrive, hold them near.

The Cry of a Distant Dawn

As the first light breaks the gloom,
The world awakens, dispels the doom.
Colors burst, a vibrant array,
Welcoming in a brand new day.

Birds chirp sweetly, a joyful song,
Echoing where hearts belong.
With each sunrise, dreams renew,
In every ray, hope shines through.

Gentle breezes carry cheer,
Gathering friends from far and near.
With open hearts, we celebrate,
As morning's glow calls us to fate.

So dance, rejoice beneath the sky,
For every moment, let laughter fly.
In the cry of dawn's embrace,
Festivity finds a sacred space.

Whispers of the Untamed

In the woods where laughter flows,
Colors dance, a vibrant show.
Joy spills out from every tree,
Embracing all who dare to be.

Under starry skies we roam,
Chasing dreams, we find our home.
With each whisper in the night,
Magic twirls in pure delight.

The Night's Veil of Solitude

In shadows deep, the stars appear,
Softly glowing, drawing near.
A gentle hush, the world at rest,
Inviting all to feel their best.

A single candle's flickering flame,
Whispers secrets, calls our name.
In quiet moments, hearts unite,
Wrapped in peace, a warm, sweet light.

Shadows of a Fading Hearth

Once a blaze that brightly burned,
Now just embers fondly turned.
Memories linger, tales of old,
In the warmth, our joy unfolds.

Gathered close, we share our cheer,
Laughter echoes, drawing near.
In the glow of love's embrace,
We find our home, our sacred space.

Beneath the Frosty Canopy

Snowflakes twirl, a dance so light,
Crystals glimmer in the night.
Laughter sings through frosty air,
Warming hearts beyond compare.

Underneath the boughs so bright,
Winter's charm ignites delight.
Together we'll make memories,
Beneath the chill, we're filled with ease.

Paths Untaken in the Glade

In the glade where laughter spills,
Joyful echoes in the air,
Footprints dance on dewy hills,
Whispers weave without a care.

Colors twirl like autumn leaves,
Sunlight dapples on the ground,
Every heart here boldly believes,
Each delight more profound.

Songs of chirping crickets play,
Crisp and clear beneath the trees,
Twilight calls the end of day,
While fireflies light the breeze.

Paths untaken, stories wait,
In the glade where spirits soar,
Gather round, don't hesitate,
Let the night reveal much more.

The Void Where the Pack Once Roamed

Amidst the echoes of the wild,
The moonlight dances, soft and bright,
Where shadows played and wolves once smiled,
Now whispers linger in the night.

Stars above with stories old,
Trace the trails of those who strayed,
In the quiet, memories unfold,
Of joyous howls of freedom played.

But in the hush, a heartbeat thuds,
A longing stirs in deep recess,
For laughter lost beneath the buds,
And bonds of fur and tenderness.

Though absence lingers, peace remains,
In silent gatherings of souls,
For every void that love contains,
Leaves space for new, magical goals.

Among the Treetops, Lonely Thoughts

High above, where branches weave,
A world unfolds in leafy dreams,
Among the treetops, hearts believe,
In silent hopes and whispered schemes.

Dances of the breezes play,
Chasing shadows, laughing low,
In the sunlight's warm display,
Each brightly hued leaf seems to glow.

Yet in the quiet, thoughts may roam,
Seeking solace in the sway,
Among the boughs, I find my home,
In fleeting moments, dreams can stay.

Here, high above the worldly strife,
The spirit soars, unbound and free,
In nature's arms, I taste sweet life,
Among the treetops, joy's decree.

Fragments of Moonlit Yearning

Under the blanket of the night,
Silver beams cast gentle grace,
Dreams drift softly, taking flight,
In moonlit whispers, hearts embrace.

Fragments of a world so sweet,
Dancing light on rippling streams,
With every pulse, the stars repeat,
Echoes of our secret dreams.

In the dark, hope finds its way,
Through every shadow, every sigh,
Holding on to night's ballet,
As wishes float across the sky.

Yearning stirs in quiet night,
Where hearts align and spirits soar,
In the moonlit realm of light,
We find our love forevermore.

Howling at the Silent Stars

Beneath the moon's soft glow we stand,
Our laughter dances, hand in hand.
Stars shimmer bright, a joyful tune,
We howl together, beneath the moon.

With every echo, our spirits rise,
A chorus caught in midnight skies.
The world alive with blissful cheer,
In this moment, we feel no fear.

The night is young, our hearts beat loud,
We celebrate, beneath the shroud.
Let whispers of dreams fill the air,
As we join the stars, beyond compare.

Together we weave a tapestry bright,
Crafting memories in the night.
Howling at dreams that never fade,
In the silence, our joy is made.

Alone in the Midnight Forest

The trees stand tall, and shadows play,
As midnight whispers lead the way.
Stars peek through the canopy high,
In solitude, I breathe the sigh.

The night's embrace, a gentle friend,
With every rustle, the fears suspend.
Crickets sing their lullaby sweet,
Echoing the rhythm of heartbeat.

Moonlit paths invite my feet,
Every step feels wild and fleet.
In the arms of night, I find my muse,
A dance of shadows, I gladly choose.

Though alone, I'm never quite lost,
In the forest's song, there is no cost.
A festive spirit, I cherish thus,
In this midnight world, it's just us.

A Lonesome Pursuit under Celestial Skies

With lanterns bright, I roam the night,
Chasing dreams, in pure delight.
Celestial bodies twinkle and sway,
Guiding my heart, showing the way.

Each step a dance, a joyful thrill,
As whispers of stars give me a chill.
The cosmos hums a tranquil tune,
In my quest, I feel the moon.

Though lonesome paths might greet my stride,
Festive sparks ignite inside.
For every star, a wish takes flight,
Painting the canvas of the night.

Together with shadows, I make my trace,
In every corner, a warm embrace.
A lonesome pursuit, but oh so grand,
Under celestial skies, I make my stand.

The Lonely Trail of the Wild Spirit

In the wild, where whispers call,
I find a peace, a spirit enthralled.
The path ahead, a ribbon of light,
Guides me softly through the night.

Each moment hums with earthy grace,
The stars above my only trace.
Through valleys deep and mountains high,
I roam alone, I spread my wings wide.

Yet in the silence, I feel the joy,
Each rustling leaf, nature's toy.
The loneliness sings a festive tune,
In the heart of night, I find my boon.

The trail I walk, an endless quest,
With every heartbeat, I am blessed.
The wild spirit dances, free and bold,
In the lonely trail, adventures unfold.

Solitary Footprints in the Snow

Footprints dance on winter's white,
Sparkling under moon's soft light.
Each step whispers tales of cheer,
As laughter floats, the night draws near.

Snowflakes swirl in festive air,
Starlit nights, beyond compare.
A chilly breeze, a heart aglow,
Secrets held where soft winds blow.

Candles flicker in the dark,
Each glowing flame a hopeful spark.
Together, hearts in joy conspire,
As warmth ignites our winter fire.

A toast to dreams and love's embrace,
In every footprint, find your place.
In silent woods, where echoes play,
Festive joy will find its way.

A Heartbeat Among the Hollow Trees

Beneath the branches, shadows spread,
Life beats softly, love is fed.
In hollow trees, the whispers flow,
Echoes dance to a festive show.

Leaves aflame with colors bright,
Each heartbeat brings a spark of light.
In the breeze, laughter hints and weaves,
A melody among the leaves.

Joyful sounds weave through the night,
A tapestry of pure delight.
Each pulse within the solemn wood,
Tells stories of the merry good.

Gathered close, let spirits soar,
Among the trees, we'll sing once more.
In nature's arms, we find our glee,
A heartbeat strong, forever free.

Echoes of a Forgotten Pack

Howls beneath the silver skies,
Echoes rich with festive sighs.
Memories of laughter undulate,
In moonlit nights, we celebrate.

The pack once roamed through fields of light,
In every heart, a bond so tight.
Lost voices now in shadows play,
Yet joy remains to guide our way.

With every echo, stories blend,
Through ancient woods where legends end.
We raise our voices, bold and clear,
In unity, we hold them near.

Resounding joy in night's embrace,
Reminds us of our sacred place.
Forgotten pack, yet not alone,
In festive echoes, we have grown.

Whispers Beneath the Boughs

Beneath the boughs where secrets sway,
Joyful whispers greet the day.
In verdant realms where shadows play,
Festive spirits lead the way.

Petals flutter, colors bright,
Nature hums a tune of light.
Each gentle breeze, a happy sigh,
Invites the heart to dance and fly.

Gather 'round where warmth abounds,
Laughter rings in joyous sounds.
Life's sweet moments tightly bound,
In nature's arms, lost souls found.

As twilight falls, let praises rise,
With cheerful hearts, we claim the skies.
In every whisper, let us know,
Together here, the love will grow.